THE BEST DOGS EVER

PORTUGUESE WATER DOGS ARE THE BEST!

Elaine Landau

LERNER PUBLICATIONS COMPANY · MINNEAPOLIS

For Carl Harvey

Lerner Publications Company
A division of Lerner Publishing Group, Inc.
241 First Avenue North
Minneapolis, MN 55401 U.S.A.

Website address: www.lernerbooks.com

Library of Congress Cataloging-in-Publication Data

Landau, Elaine.
    Portuguese water dogs are the best! / by Elaine Landau.
        p.   cm. – (The best dogs ever)
    Includes index.
    ISBN 978-0-7613-5060-6 (lib. bdg. : alk. paper)
    1. Portuguese water dog. I. Title.
  SF429.P87L36 2010
  636.73–dc22   2009012987

Manufactured in the United States of America
1 2 3 4 5 6 – BP – 15 14 13 12 11 10

TABLE OF CONTENTS

CHAPTER ONE
THE IDEAL DOG

What's your ideal dog? Would it be a big dog with as much energy as you? How about a pooch that's playful and curious? Or would you like a dog with lots of smarts and true-blue loyalty?

What if all these things appeal to you? Then your ideal pooch just may be a **Portuguese water dog!**

Portuguese water dogs are called PWDs for short. These dogs can be tons of fun. They also make great pets.

PWDs are spirited dogs that make great companions for active families.

So Cute to Boot!

PWDs are good-looking dogs too. Have you ever seen one up close? You might think you were looking at an overgrown fluff ball.

NAMING YOUR NEW DOG

Every super dog needs a name it can be proud of. Would your PWD happily come when called if you gave it any of these names?

Captain

Bella

Gatsby

Jewel

MAGELLAN

Buddy

Chloe

JAZZY

Curley

Lily

A male PWD stands about 22 inches (56 centimeters) tall at the shoulder. It can weigh as much as 60 pounds (27 kilograms). That's about the weight of an eight-year-old boy. Imagine picking up a third grader. That's what it would be like to lift a full-grown male PWD.

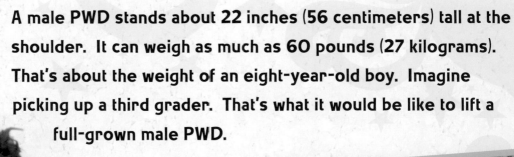

PWDs are large enough to keep up with their owners on long walks.

Female PWDs tend to be a little smaller. They are about 19 inches (48 cm) tall at the shoulder. They weigh up to 50 pounds (23 kg). That's about the weight of a six-year-old girl.

Some PWDs have short, curly coats.
Others have medium-length wavy
coats. PWDs come in different colors
too. These dogs may be black, white,
or brown. Many are also black and
white or brown and white.

This PWD puppy is wearing a safety vest as it swims in a lake.

Portuguese water dogs love water. But you probably guessed that from their name. They are super swimmers. Like ducks, PWDs have webbed feet. Webbed feet help the dogs swim.

A FIRST DOG FOR THE FIRST FAMILY

In April 2009, President Barack Obama's family got its first dog. This very special White House pet is a black-and-white PWD. The Obama daughters, eleven-year-old Malia and eight-year-old Sasha, named the new puppy Bo. Bo Diddley was a popular rock-and-roll singer in the 1950s and 1960s—and Michelle Obama's father's nickname was Diddley. So the name Bo seemed like the perfect fit. Malia and Sasha also have cousins who have a cat named Bo.

A Curly Best Friend

PWDs are a joy to have around. They love spending time with their human family. They seem to think they're one of the kids! Their owners think PWDs are the best dogs ever.

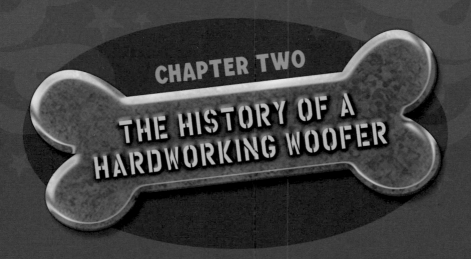

CHAPTER TWO
THE HISTORY OF A HARDWORKING WOOFER

A PWD is more than a pleasant pooch. It is also a hardworking dog. For hundreds of years, these dogs helped people in Portugal catch fish. They swam and dived to do so.

PWDs not only caught fish. They also brought up torn fishing nets. They carried messages between boats. At night, they guarded the boat and the day's catch. These canines did not tire easily.

SAME DOG, DIFFERENT NAME

In Portugal, PWDs are called Cao de Agua. This means "water dog."

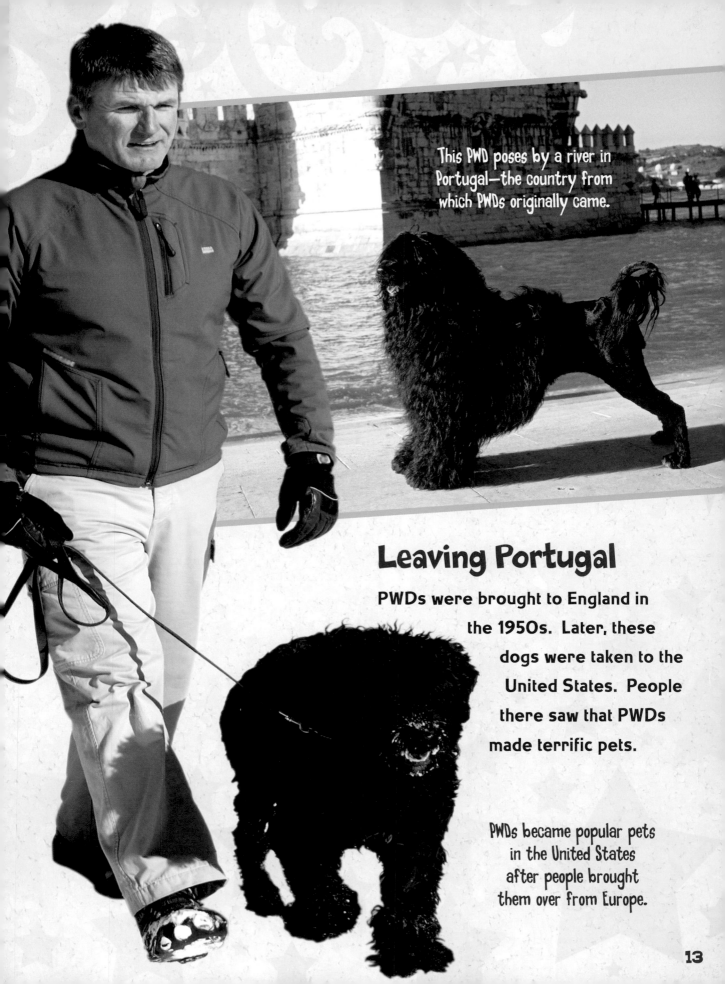

This PWD poses by a river in Portugal—the country from which PWDs originally came.

Leaving Portugal

PWDs were brought to England in the 1950s. Later, these dogs were taken to the United States. People there saw that PWDs made terrific pets.

PWDs became popular pets in the United States after people brought them over from Europe.

A PEANUT-SNIFFING PWD

Some PWDs still work in modern times. Among them is a dog named Rock'O. Rock'O has been trained to sniff out peanuts. He is one of only six dogs in the United States that can do this.

Peanut-sniffing dogs help children with serious peanut allergies. These kids can't even be near peanuts. When a peanut-sniffing dog smells a peanut, it might stop an allergic child from entering the room. Then a nonallergic person can go into the room and remove the peanut so the child can be safe.

In 1972, sixteen PWD owners started the Portuguese Water Dog Club of America. As PWDs became more popular, more and more people joined the club. These days, the club has more than one thousand members!

The Working Group

The American Kennel Club (AKC) groups dogs by breed. Breeds that are alike in some ways are grouped together. Some of the AKC's groups are the toy group, the herding group, and the hound group.

PWDs are in the working group. All the dogs in this group are strong and smart. They are also pretty big.

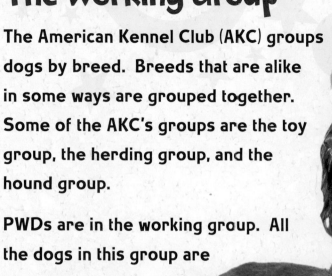

German shepherds (*left*) are in the herding group, while Yorkshire terriers (*below*) are in the toy group.

This Afghan hound is in the hound group.

CHAPTER THREE
THE RIGHT DOG FOR YOU

What if you could get any dog you wished for? Would you wish for a PWD? Who wouldn't want such a cute pooch for a pal?

PWD LOVERS

Senator Ted Kennedy's family loves PWDs. They have three of them named Splash, Sunny, and Cappy. The senator sometimes takes his dogs to work with him. They have been seen sleeping under his desk. They've also gone to some very important meetings!

Senator Kennedy wanted the Obamas to have a PWD too. The new presidential pup, Bo, was a gift from him. Bo is from the same litter as the senator's dog Cappy.

Senator Ted Kennedy of Massachusetts speaks to a crowd while Sunny and Splash stand by.

But be careful what you wish for! Not every dog is right for everyone. Keep reading to see if a PWD is the pet for you.

Do you like watching TV more than playing outdoors? If so, don't get a PWD. These hardy dogs have loads of energy. They need at least an hour of daily exercise.

PWDs need lots of exercise every day.

This energetic PWD plays tug-of-war in the snow with his owner.

How busy are you? Do you have lots of after-school activities? Do the grown-ups who care for you work outside the home?

PWDs don't do well at home alone. They always want to be with the humans they love. Think hard before getting any dog. Do you really have time for one? If not, a bird or a fish might be a better pet for you.

PWDs like to be around their owners. They don't want to be alone all day.

Are you willing to spend time grooming your dog?
PWDs need lots of grooming. You'll have to brush
your dog often. Most PWD owners also take their
dogs to a professional groomer. This can be costly.
Make sure your family can afford it.

PWD Pluses

If you have the time, money, and energy for a PWD, then you're lucky. These dogs have lots of pluses. They're good-natured, and they love to please. They also have a single coat. This means they have just one layer of fur. Single-coated dogs don't shed much. Many people with allergies do quite well with them.

If a PWD is the pooch for you, get set for a wonderful time. A big bundle of love and fun is coming your way!

A PERFECT MATCH

Bo is a perfect match for the Obamas. Malia (left, with Bo) has allergies, so she needs a dog that doesn't shed a lot. Bo is also a first-rate charmer and quite well behaved.

The dog worked with a trainer before coming to the White House. This was important because PWDs have lots of energy. They need to be properly trained. No one wants to see the nation's first dog racing through the White House or tearing up the Rose Garden. Bo Obama looks like a classy dog and acts like one too.

CHAPTER FOUR

HERE COMES YOUR POOCH!

Today's the day you've waited for. You're getting your PWD! Have your camera ready. You'll want pictures. Be ready in other ways too. Have the things you'll need to make your new dog feel at home.

Not sure what you'll need to welcome Fido to your family? This basic list is a great place to start:

- collar

- leash

- tags (for identification)

- dog food

- food and water bowls

- crates (one for when your pet travels by car and one for it to rest in at home)

- treats (to be used in training)

- toys

This PWD still has the blue eyes that many puppies are born with. The eyes later change to a darker color.

See a Vet

Take your new dog to a veterinarian soon. That's a doctor who treats animals. They are sometimes called vets for short.

This vet is pointing out a break in a dog's leg bone. Vets help you keep your dog healthy.

The vet will check your dog to be sure it's healthy. Your dog will also get the shots it needs. You'll be back at the vet's office again. Take your dog there for checkups. Also take your dog to the vet if it becomes ill.

Puppies need different foods than older dogs. Your vet can help you figure out which foods will make your PWD healthy and strong.

DOGGIE DINING

Ask your vet what to feed your PWD. Your dog will need different food at different times in its life. Don't give your dog table scraps. This can lead to an unhealthful weight gain.

Get Ready to Groom

PWDs have beautiful coats. But they need lots of grooming to look their best. Brush your dog at least three times a week. This will remove any dead hair. It will also help stop matting, or severe tangling.

This PWD is getting groomed before a dog show. All PWDs need grooming.

You and Your Dog

A PWD is a very special dog. It's up to you to make it feel loved. Spend lots of time with your pooch. Take your PWD to a park or open field. Play ball or fetch with it. A game of Frisbee is fun too.

Your PWD will also enjoy hiking with you. Do you swim at a nearby lake? Your dog will love swimming with you and playing in the water.

Just as their name suggests, Portuguese water dogs love the water.

A LIFETIME OF LOVE

With good food and care, your PWD should live from ten to fifteen years. Make these happy years for both of you.

You'll always be the center of your dog's world. It will depend on you for all its needs. Don't let your PWD down. Be your dog's best friend. Take pride in caring for it. Having a dog is a big responsibility. Show your PWD that you're up to the task.

GLOSSARY

American Kennel Club (AKC): an organization that groups dogs by breed. The AKC also defines the characteristics of different breeds.

breed: a particular type of dog. Dogs of the same breed have the same body shape and general features.

canine: a dog or having to do with dogs

coat: a dog's fur

groom: to clean, brush, and trim a dog's coat

matting: severe tangling. Matting causes fur to clump together in large masses.

shed: to lose fur

veterinarian: a doctor who treats animals. Veterinarians are called vets for short.

webbed: connected by a web or fold of skin

working group: a group of dogs that were bred to do different types of jobs, such as guarding property, carrying messages, or pulling sleds

FOR MORE INFORMATION

Books

Brecke, Nicole, and Patricia M. Stockland. *Dogs You Can Draw*. Minneapolis: Millbrook Press, 2010. Perfect for dog lovers, this colorful book teaches readers how to draw many different popular dog breeds.

Landau, Elaine. *Your Pet Dog*. Rev. ed. New York: Children's Press, 2007. This title is a good guide for young people on choosing and caring for a dog.

Lewis, J. Patrick, and Beth Zappitello. *First Dog*. Chelsea, MI: Sleeping Bear Press, 2009. This fun story is all about a dog's long search for the perfect home. Can you guess how the story ends?

Markle, Sandra. *Animal Heroes: True Rescue Stories*. Minneapolis: Millbrook Press, 2009. Markle tells how dogs and other animals have helped humans in dangerous situations.

O'Sullivan, Robyn. *More Than Man's Best Friend: The Story of Working Dogs*. Washington, DC: National Geographic, 2006. Profiles of various working dogs are featured in this book. Readers will enjoy learning about these clever canines and the tasks they perform.

Websites

American Kennel Club
http://www.akc.org
Visit this website to find a complete listing of AKC-registered dog breeds, including the Portuguese water dog. This site also features fun printable activities for kids.

FBI Working Dogs
http://www.fbi.gov/kids/dogs/doghome.htm
This fun site explains all about working dogs and tells how canine crime fighters help the FBI.

Index

Photo Acknowledgments

The images in this book are used with the permission of: © Cheryl Erteit/Visuals Unlimited, Inc., p. 4; © Christopher Furlong/Getty Images, p. 5 (left); © Deborah Lee Miller/The Image Works, pp. 5 (right), 9 (inset), 20-21, 28 (inset); © Fiona Green, pp. 6 (left), 14 (bottom); © Bonnie Sue Rauch/Photo Researchers, Inc., pp. 6-7; © Larry Reynolds/dogpix.com, pp. 7 (right), 12, 16, 24 (top), 28 (main); © Bob Shirtz/SuperStock, p. 8 (top); © Jerry Shulman/SuperStock, pp. 8-9; © Sharon Montrose/The Image Bank/Getty Images, p. 9 (main); The White House, p. 10 (top); Reflexstock/First Light/Brian Summers, p. 10 (bottom); © Manon Ringuette/Dreamstime.com, pp. 11, 13 (left), 18 (bottom), 27 (top); © Juniors Bildarchiv/Alamy, p. 13 (right); © Chuck Bigger/USA TODAY, p. 14 (top); © iStockphoto.com/Kevin Russ, p. 15 (left); © iStockphoto.com/Eric Isselée, p. 15 (right); AP Photo/Robert F. Bukaty, p. 17 (top); © Lisa Wiley/The Image Works, p. 17 (bottom), 18 (top), 23 (bottom), 25 (top), 29; © Joy Brown/Shutterstock Images, p. 19 (top); © iStockphoto.com/Lee Feldstein, p. 19 (bottom); © John Daniels/ardea.com, p. 20 (left); AP Photo/Ron Edmonds, p. 21 (bottom); © Zottelhund-Fotolia.com, p. 22; © Tooties/Dreamstime.com, p. 23 (top); © Uturnpix/Dreamstime.com, p. 23 (second from top); © iStockphoto.com/orix3, p. 23 (third from top); © Apple Tree House/Lifesize/Getty Images, p. 24 (bottom); © Robyn Mackenzie/Shutterstock Images, p. 25 (bottom); AP Photo/Mary Altaffer, p. 26 (top); © Tristan Hawke/Alamy, p. 26-27.

Front cover: © Alan Merrigan/Shuterstock Images.
Back cover: © Thomas Photography LLC/Alamy.